Please Don't Crush!

First paperback edition May 2024

ISBN: 979-8-9861997-7-1

Also available in paperback.

Author website: kturnerauthor.com

Wait!

Please don't put me in that jar.
A group of fireflies may be referred to as a "sparkle,"
a "light show," or a "swarm."

This field is my home, and I don't like to travel very far.

My name is Flick, and I'm a firefly as you can see.

An insect is a small animal whose body is divided into three parts. Insects also have three pairs of legs, and usually one or two pairs of wings.

And it's very, very cool to be an insect like me.

This is because fireflies are bioluminescent, meaning we can produce our own light.

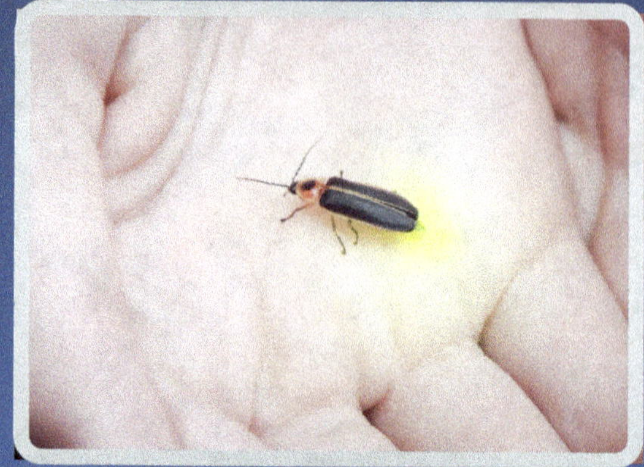

And this sure comes in handy when
we're flying around at night.

Now you may be wondering where we go when the sun comes up and it's time for you to play.

So I'll let you in on a little secret.

In the tall grass is where we like to

spend our day.

As an insect, our body consists of...

6 legs,

4 wings,

3 body parts, and

2 antennae on top of our head.

And since our outer pair of wings are hardened, we're actually a member of the beetle family.

That's right! The beetle family is what I said.

(European Rhinoceros Beetle)

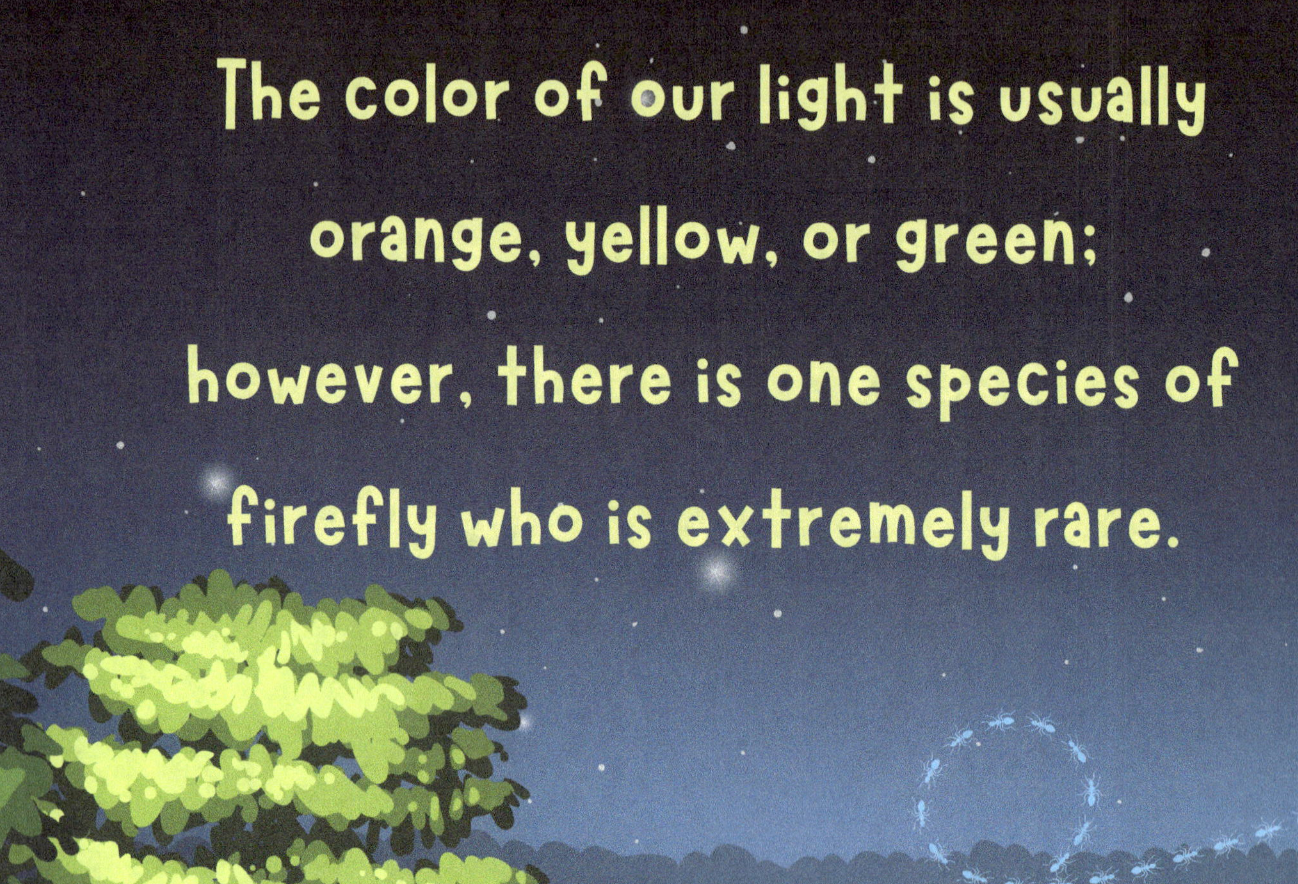
The color of our light is usually orange, yellow, or green; however, there is one species of firefly who is extremely rare.

They can flash the color blue as they go gliding through the air.
The blue ghost firefly can only be found in the eastern and central United States. While other species of fireflies flash off and on, the blue ghost firefly can glow for up to a minute at a time.

Our lights not only brighten up the night, they also help us to find a mate.
To determine gender you will need to catch the firefly. A male's light organs are in the last 2 segments of their abdomen, where as females are only in the 2nd to last segment.

But we also use our flashes in order to find our way, and to help us communicate.

I bet you never would have guessed

that there is over

2000

species of fireflies in the world,

though not all of them glow.

The ones who don't use pheromones (their sense of smell) in determining where they should go.

Have you ever wondered how it is that we can glow?

Luciferin is the light emitting compound found in organisms that generate bioluminescence when an enzyme called Luciferase is present.

There's a chemical in our light organ

called Luciferin which helps us put

on our nighttime show.

Our babies, known as larva, are carnivores. This means that their diet consists of eating meat.

As a defense, firefly larva may glow to let other predators know that they do not taste good.

But as adults, it's the nectar and pollen from plants that we like to eat.

Because of this, some species of fireflies can be effective pollinators. This means they help plants produce and grow.

So remember to say thank you when your fruits and vegetables are popping up in a row.

Unfortunately, the firefly population has been declining due to factors such as habitat destruction.

As well as the

use of

pesticides,

AND

of course, light

disruption.

So, what can you do to help the firefly population out?

Say no to harmful pesticides,

turn off the lights when you're not using them,

and leave us some tall grass scattered about.

And whatever you do, when you reach out with your hands to give us a brush...

Some species of fireflies release toxic chemicals, known as lucibufagins, which are poisonous to predators.

Please
don't crush!

Glossary

Antennae

A pair of long, thin body parts located on the head, which are used to feel and smell.

Bioluminescent

The biochemical emission of light by living organisms.

Carnivore

An organism that eats mostly meat.

Insect

A small animal whose body is divided into three parts. Insects also have three pairs of legs and usually one or two pairs of wings.

Luciferin

The light emitting compound found in organisms that generate bioluminescence when an enzyme called Luciferase is present.

Nocturnal

Active at night as opposed to during the day.

Pheromones

A chemical substance produced and released into the environment by an animal, affecting the behavior of others in its species.

Pollinate

To move or carry pollen to a plant, causing the seeds to be fertilized.

Life Cycle of a Firefly

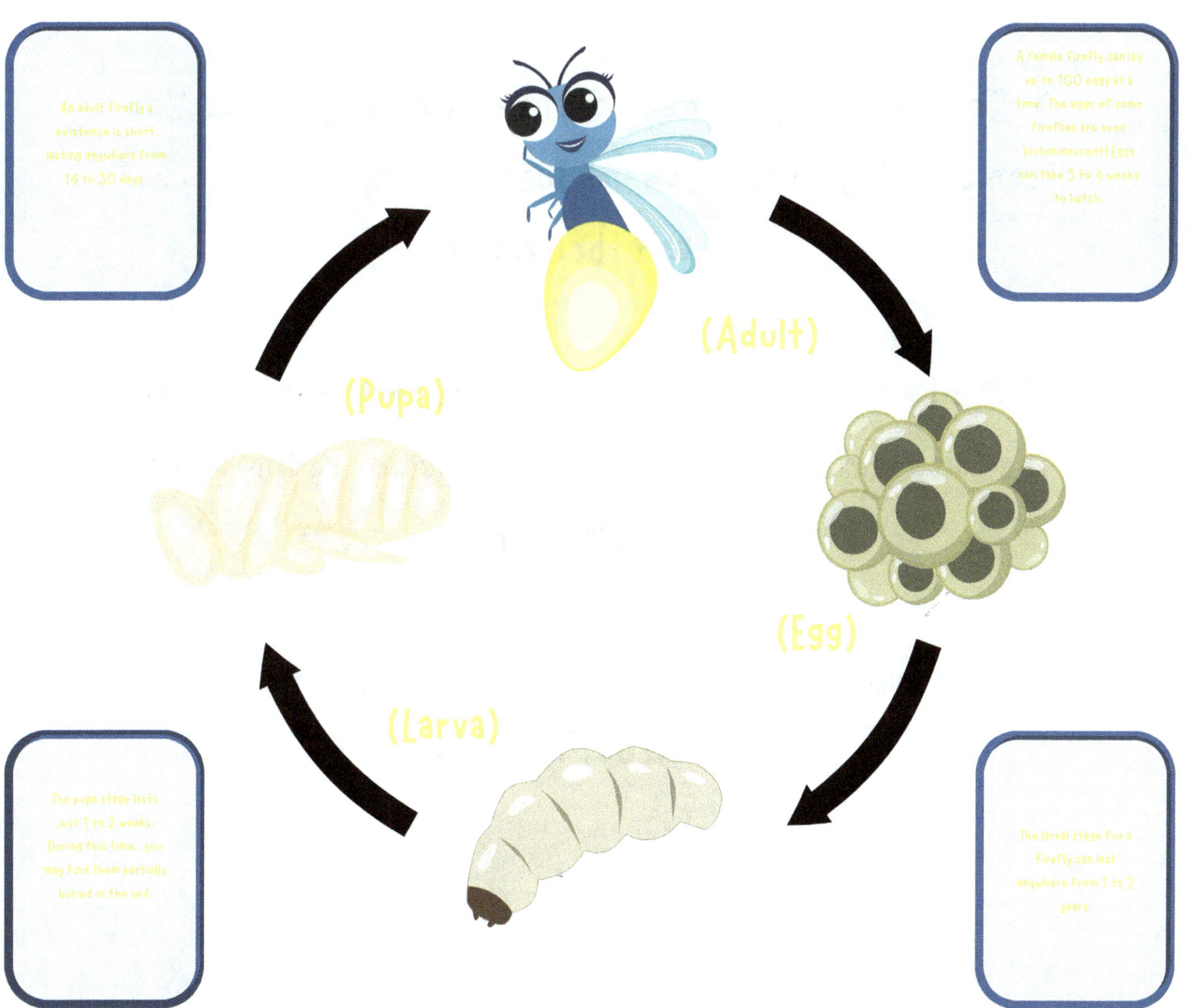

Firefly Activities for Children

1. Go on a firefly hunt and count how many you see. You can even try to catch them. Just remember to observe only, and then release.

2. Plant a garden with plenty of firefly friendly flowers. They also thrive in moist areas, so consider adding a pond or a birdbath.

3. Visit your local library to do research and learn even more about fireflies.

Discover more titles by the same author @kturnerauthor.com

Including these, and more!